Untold Stories of an Unforgotten Soul

A Guru to Many Loved Ones
Bimal Kumar Hazarika

Former OIL Indian (Oil India Limited)

and

AOCian (Assam Oil Corporation)

Untold Stories of an Unforgotten Soul

Binita Hazarika Dutta

MEMOIR: *Edition 1*

ZORBA BOOKS

ZORBA BOOKS

Published by Zorba Books, October 2021

Website: www.zorbabooks.com
Email: info@zorbabooks.com

Author Name & Copyright © Binita Hazarika Dutta

Title :- Untold Stories of an Unforgotten Soul

Print book ISBN - 978-93-90640-82-9
Ebook ISBN - 978-93-90640-90-4

The publisher under the guidance and direction of the author has published the contents in this book, and the publisher takes no responsibility for the contents, its accuracy, completeness, any inconsistencies, or the statements made. The contents of the book do not reflect the opinion of the publisher or the editor. The publisher and editor shall not be liable for any errors, omissions, or the reliability of the contents of the book.

Any perceived slight against any person/s, place or organization is purely unintentional.

Zorba Books Pvt. Ltd. (opc)
Sushant Arcade,
Next to Courtyard Marriot,
Sushant Lok 1, Gurgaon – 122009, India

Late Bimal Kumar Hazarika

Lost a long battle to cancer and left for his eternal journey on 18th July 1998.

Chief Guest Rongali Bihu

1979 Duliajan Assam

*"When you are content to be simply yourself and don't compare
or compete, everybody will respect you."*

\- Lau Tzu

Table of Contents

Preface

This is my first ever attempt at writing. Usually, novice writers spend expansive time ruminating over the idea of their first book. But I consider myself fortunate as I did not have a second thought on the content of the book.

I have a treasure trove of memories of someone close to my heart; my dear Father (Deuta), whom I lost at a very young age. All I needed to do was carve those into black and white.

So, here I am, sharing the remembrances of my Father 22 years after he answered God's final call. However, his recalls are still fresh, like lily, in the folder of my memory.

With utmost regards, I thank the below former Oil Indian who fondly remember my Father as Bimal da/ dada /*Kakaidow (Dada*/Kakaidow means **Big Brother** in Assamese). Although these dignified people were my Father's colleagues, but they have nothing been less than family members. They have been the caregivers right from the time I was born to my growing years. I express my gratitude to them for taking out time and sharing some unforgettable memories and stories about my Father.

Though he is not physically present with us, but I was overwhelmed and grateful to know he is still alive in the thoughts and memories of those who still cherish the moments they shared with him. For Deuta (Father) Oil India Limited was his home and everyone was his family.

Mr. Abani Barua
Mr. Siddarth Deb
Mr. Biren Das
Mr. Santikam Hazarika
Mr. Puna Borgohain
Mr. Swadhin Hazarika
Mr. Manas Bordoloi
Mr. Ajit Mahanta
Mr. Pradip Alley

I also thank my husband Alakesh Dutta, who encouraged me to thread the memories of my Father into a book. It is only because of Alakesh's unwavering support and contribution that has given life to this book.

This is emphatically not a typical biography. It is more of a journey of Father's life at his workplace, Oil India Limited and Assam oil Company. This book is about his passion for his profession; Crude Oil Drilling. This book is about how intellectually brilliant, emotional and warm-hearted Man he was.

Some dates and details are missing in the pictures/ write-up as they are more than 50 yrs. old.

The rest the of shared facts and information are to the best of my knowledge. Any discrepancies found should be informed, which shall be corrected in the next edition.

Introduction

It has been almost 21 yrs. since I left Assam. Thereafter, I have spent most of my life in North India (Delhi and Gurugram) for work, and then settling down with my husband after marriage. It was during the lockdown (covid-19 pandemic) when I was leafing through the old albums and recalling the moments of my childhood. Those are the recollections of my late Father, which are most precious and very close to my heart.

It has been over two decades since my Father lost his battle to lung cancer. However, the void of his absence still makes me feel weak whenever I think about him.

During the initial spell of this writing journey, I was actually not sure from where to start as my Father had already spent a certain phase of his life in the organization (Oil India Limited) Duliajan Assam before I was born. Prior to that, he worked for (Assam Oil Company) Digboi Assam, which is now the AOD (Assam Oil Division) Of IOCL INDIAN OIL CORPORATION LIMITED. But I grew up listening about his work and achievements which he used to share with me.

The tributes by some of the former Oil Indian say it all about my Father's passion, achievements, expertise, knowledge of his work as an Oil Driller. The words also eulogize his sheer presence and charismatic personality. Some of them have also shared individually their experience of working with my Father on different projects.

His discipline, leadership, and his love for his colleagues and juniors did enthuse many of them to make him their life's first Guru. The laurels sing paeans of his charisma.

This book is an attempt to share a story of an exceptional Man who not only loved but also worshiped his profession. There was a strange and powerful energy form he always convoyed with him.

The book time-travels to the moments when Deuta was posted in Bhubaneswar in the early 80s; when I started my schooling. It was during those growing-up years when my Father used to share many stories and incidents about his work; both offshore and onshore oil drilling.

He would often show me the photographs of the well sites and his workplace, how he and his team used to work together for days and nights to achieve targets. Though I don't remember the dates and details of some photographs and events (also shared in this book), but yes, he always used to cherish and live those moments.

I hope the book offers the portrait of a fascinating and deeply mystic Human Being.

Chapter One

Sneek Peek in journey from AOC (Assam Oil Company) Digboi to OIL (Oil India Limited) Duliajan

Digboi is a town in the Tinsukia district in the north-eastern part of the state of Assam, India.

Crude oil was discovered here in Digboi in the late 19th century and the first Oil well was dug in 1866. Digboi is known as the Oil City of Assam where the first Oil well in Asia was drilled. The first refinery was started here as early as 1901. Digboi has the oldest Oil Well in operation. A significant number of British professionals worked for Assam Oil Company until the decade following the Independence of India.

As per the information shared by Mr. D. N Chalia (former AOCian and OIL Indian), whom I fondly address as Uncle, my Father Late Bimal Kumar Hazarika joined AOC in Digboi back in November 1957, exactly two months after Mr. Chalia (uncle) joined, that is on 16th Sep 1957. In no time, my Father became a perfectionist and a diligent achiever as an Oil Driller in AOC Digboi. He was considered one of the most highly experienced and exceptional person.

Duliajan is an industrial town located in the Dibrugarh district in the upper north-east tuft of India. It is particularly known for its oil-related industry, Oil India Limited, one of the country's largest oil and gas companies. Assam Gas Company Limited, which carries out business related to natural gas in India, owned by the Government of Assam, is also located in this township.

A nucleus of experienced personnel is drawn from AOC as well as BOC (Burmah Oil Company), entitling it as the pioneer of Digboi Oilfield. Oil India formally set up its organization in 1962 to look after all the aspects of drilling and exploration operations, with its headquarter in Duliajan, then known as Zaloni in the Naharkatiya area. It was a 50% Central Govt undertaking and 50% BOC undertaking.

My Father, uncle D.N Chalia and the rest of the team received their transfer confirmation from AOC to the newly formed OIL INDIA LIMITED on 1st Jan 1962. (As told by Chalia Uncle over the telephonic conversation in 2020)

They were the first group of Oil Drilling Engineers and experienced personals who joined Oil India and worked like a Trojan to explore the Oil fields in Naharkatiya Moran, Kharsang to name a few. **Oil India Limited was born in front of them (AS THEY PROUDLY EXCLAIM).** Father was looked upon as one of the most tireless and self-driven people in his work. In 1981, OIL was completely undertaken by the Central Government.

Today, elaborately, OIL works in varied fields like Exploration of crude Oil and Natural Gas, Pipe Line Production and Transportation, Electric Power Generation, LPG Production.

Chapter Two

About my Father (Deuta)

The early days of his childhood was full of struggles. Of 9 children, he was the eldest. Needless to mention; financial constraint was always an issue with a stack of responsibilities to be shouldered, being the eldest.

Those struggles had influenced him to the nth degree and transformed him into the man he was. And that's the reason he always taught how to live within one's means and the values of sharing and caring.

Science would always light up his eyes. He could solve problems of maths and physics in the blink of an eye. Though I was not a science lover, so after my school and tuition, I had to learn mathematics and physics from him. The guest room of our then bungalow number F-33 of Duliajan Oil Town was converted to a small classroom with blackboard chalk, duster, etc. where he used to teach, and seriously, there was no escape. (Recalling the moment when he took me to a glass shop and bought some rectangular and triangular-shaped mirrors to make my first mid-school project; a Kaleidoscope.)

After passing out from Digboi Boys School with double distinction in Mathematics and Science, he joined Cotton College, Guwahati, Assam for his higher studies where he excelled in his favorite subjects Mathematics Physics and Chemistry.

If I have to describe him today, in few words, it would be:

A highbrow mentor in Mathematics. (Though I was not inclined to Mathematics, but he taught me several practicable techniques and analysis when I was buckling up for the competitive exams. After his death, needless to say, I missed him terribly while I was preparing).

He strongly believed and taught what once the great Indian Mathematician Shakuntala Devi quoted–

"Without Mathematics, there is nothing you can do Everything around you is Mathematics. Everything around you is numbers."

- An absolute sports enthusiast - a soccer lover (Once he shared that he was the captain of his school football team, Digboi Boys School) and also he had a keen interest for playing lawn tennis and badminton.

He always encouraged me for sports. So, during my school and college days, I won several accolades in swimming, table tennis, badminton and many other games. I represented my school till the Zonal level in athletics. Then, in college, I won the best player award. I surely give this credit of all my achievements to my Father for all his unwavering support.

(He believed and taught that a fit mind starts with a fit body, and sports is one of the most significant ways

to teach yourself self-discipline. It can help to chase perfection in whatever you do.)

- A spectacular teacher and a true mentor, who made sure that anything you learn must be learned from scratch and you must master it.
- He was acclaimed for his knowledge, dedication, love and passion for his profession (Oil Drilling).

He said that every single challenge he faced; he made sure it turned into a golden opportunity for him to explore the potential of his work.

He was so passionate that he was beyond the boundaries of the day and night. At times, working for 24 hours a day vigorously was normal for him. He often worked in late-night shifts. I was too young at that time, but I surely remember waking up late at nights, and checking if my Father was back from his work.

During one of our (Father-daughter) conversations, he recalled traveling to several countries for his offshore training and projects in the era of 60s and 70s. He mentioned Houston, UK, Mexico, Europe (Italy, Paris Germany) and so on.

I believe going for offshore training and work in those days was a crowning achievement.

He believed that anything can be achieved as long as you have the zeal, the focus and the drive in whatever you do.

Chapter Three

Emotional and Kind-Hearted Man

Besides his strong persona, he was a very emotional and kind-hearted man.

Father was always devoted to lending a hand to others, even if that demanded going the extra mile. He religiously believed in giving back to the society. During his lifetime, he helped many people whom we (family members) did not even know.

In the early 80s, Father was posted in Bhubaneswar for one of his projects in OIL. (which is also mentioned by former Oil Indian Uncle Shatikam Hazarika in his tribute).

There, we lived in a rented independent house which had quite a big compound. The house was located in close proximity to St. Joseph High School. One of the houses adjacent to ours (besides the walls of the compound) was a very small house, they hardly had any extra space in the name of a compound. There was one old lady (I can't precisely recall as I was too young), either she was the mother or the grandmother of a girl child. And if I am not mistaken, she was a widow. Often, when Father used to come back from the office, she used to talk with him in half Hindi and half Oriya. Father, though he didn't under understand Oriya, but whatever broken Hindi the lady spoke, he could understand. The talks were basically about the girl child who was of marriageable age and, of course; they needed help as some of their relatives had denied any support. The first request from them was because their house was too small, would my Father allow them to use our house as the base for marriage purposes. Then they asked if our compound could be used for the other marriage rituals.

For a Man who could never hurt or say no to anyone, the next step was Father took was, he temporarily got some part of the boundary wall dismantled for short access to our house.

The next thing I remember is that there was a huge pandal (temporary fabricated structure for the religious ceremony) in our compound with all decorations and catering arrangements, and I am pretty sure most of the expenses were incurred by him (Father). The bride was getting ready in my room and her seating arrangements were made in the dining room. Our whole house; from the main gate to our dining room was brimful of their guests. Then the Pandit (priest), bridegroom, and his family arrived. The girl (bride) was convoyed by her family members to the pandal for Saat Pheras (Indian wedding ritual). Both took blessings of my Father and later her bidai (departure of the bride and the bride groom) was performed from our premises.

The unknown neighbor (old lady) was so grateful to him (Father) and thanked him from the bottom of her heart for all he had done for her girl child.

Later, in 1987, we shifted back to Assam and after that, we never heard about them.

There are so many instances wherein he helped myriad people in his lifetime. If I attempt to write about all those incidents, it might turn into a thick book.

I can recall another instance when a woman often used to come to our bungalow in Duliajan. She has lost her husband and both sons had refused to look after her as she grew old. Though I have blurred memories of that incident, her house was a small hut on the way to Tinsukia; a very pitiful look from the outside. Broken bamboo barriers, no lights, broken windows.

We did not know her. But someone has said to her that if she has any problem in her life, she should go to Bimal kakaidow/ Dada place. The expression dada denotes 'elder brother' and is used in terms of great respect.

I was probably 9 or 10 yrs. old at that time. When I used to look at her, she always had teary eyes. She narrated her bit of the story to Father. So whenever possible, Father helped her financially, which was nothing less than a lifeline to her.

Father was indeed a rare, generous man. There was a word spread around that if you go to Kakeidow/Dada's (Brother) place in your tough times, you will never return empty-handed and empty stomach.

Deuta believed that helping other people can be a cure, not just for those who are in need, but for your soul as well.

But as mentioned by one of the former oil Indian uncle Siddharth Deb, in his tribute, it is also true that many people took advantage of his bigheartedness in his lifetime.

Father was loved and admired by every sections of people, all starta of society, because he considered everyone to be equal and everyone at Oil India as his own family.

Back then, it felt like; I was growing up in a big, fat joint family.

While writing this bit of story, I recall when my Father, out of his four younger brothers, lost one of his most loved brothers, Late Jiten Hazarika (Uncle /Khura Atul) in a tragic road accident near Khetri on the way from Diphu to Guwahati in the year 1990. Deuta was speechless and broken. He didn't know how he would live without uncle as he was very close to him. Out of 9 siblings, uncle's death was the first and that too at a very young age.

I remember whenever we used to visit Guwahati from Duliajan (which is approximately a 10-hr. drive) for our vacations, Father used to halt at the highway spot near Khetri (mostly we would reach around late in the evening as it was near Guwahati). He would light some incense sticks, candles and offer prayers near the road where the accident took place.

It became a ritual for us to stop the car in mid of highway, Father would then offer his prayers at the accident site.

Years later, while writing this, my heart melts; at how he felt so hurt that he would pull over at the accident site every time and pray for one of his most loved brothers to rest in peace.

It was unconditional love and attachment with him (Brother).

"The soul is neither born, nor does it ever die, nor exits only once, nor it ever ceases to be. The soul is without birth, eternal, immortal and ageless. It is not destroyed when the body is destroyed." – BHAGAWAT GITA

Deuta cared and loved everyone.

There is another story that has stirred up in the folder of my memory. Probably I was 10 or 12 years old at that time (in the decade of 90s). It was monsoon time; it was thundering and raining cats and dogs that day in Duliajan Oil Town. Many people left their offices for home and fortunately, Father came home earlier.

That late evening, one of our staff came running to Father and said, "Sahab (sir) Mon Bahadur has come."

Mon Bahadur was a temporary cook, plus a gardener at our bungalow. He was also permanently working for Duliajan OIL guest house. So, whenever he got time, he used to spend time with other staff at our bungalow and also take care of the household chores. In Duliajan, each servant line was connected to four bungalows.

So that rainy night, when Mon Bahadur (I used to call him Kaka) came, I remember, both Father and Kaka running towards the servant line, to Kaka's room.

I was asked to get the Fiat car keys and be at the porch. After a few minutes of wait, I saw Father, who was over 50 years at that time, carrying Kaka's teenage son in his arms and rushing towards the car porch. His son was soaked in blood, he was bleeding from his knees and nose, his head was all swollen, his hand was broken. I somehow can't forget that dreadful scene when Father was carrying the teenage boy from the servant quarters in his arms on a heavy downpour day. He quickly managed to get the boy and Kaka in his car, and rushed to the Oil Town Hospital. When Father returned, he was barefooted because he forgot where he took off his slippers at the hospital, his whole shirt, inner garment, trousers were all stained by blood. Later, Father narrated that his son had met with an accident while learning to ride a bike. After a few days, the boy was back home after his treatment. Later, both Kaka and expressed their gratefulness to Father.

Deuta always taught to never hesitate from helping people in the time of need. That day, a delay in taking the boy to the hospital might have led to the loss of his life. Father always regretted that he was not there when his brother met with the road accident.

In another incident that happened in the late 70s, an Oil executive's wife (not mentioning the name to maintain privacy) tripped over in the Zaloni Club. The woman was 7 months pregnant. Admist the panic, Father rushed her to the Oil Town Hospital, so that both mother and child life could be saved.

"Every life is valuable. Every life matters."
— Father; Bimal Kumar Hazarika

You often imitate what you learn in your childhood. Such learnings get instilled in you without you even knowing. I realized this when, in the 2019 winters, my husband and I were on a drive at the Golf Course Road in Gurugram. Suddenly, we noticed a speeding car that just crossed us, lost its balance. It rammed into the divider and was on the tilt to topple on the other lane. In a fraction of a second, we stopped our car in the middle of the road and rushed towards the ill-fated car where the driver was stuck. He was still breathing. Fortunately, it was only him in the car. Nowadays, people usually overlook such incidents due to busyness; so much busy that human life is not a high priority anymore. As my husband and I were trying to help the driver evacuate the car, fortunately, we noticed some more helping hands approaching. Finally, when the driver was pulled out of the car, we extended our desire to take the victim to the hospital. But another greathearted man in the crowd insisted strongly and took him to the hospital. I am sure that kindhearted man must have childhood experiences of some family member being benevolent. May God bless all such people who help others in times of hardship.

This brings us to another learning; people around us, especially kids, model us. So why not perform exemplary deeds for them to follow?

"Do Something Wonderful. People may imitate it." –Albert Schweitzer (German-French Theologian) 1875-1965

Chapter Four

My Best Mentor; my Father

"Every failure must be a lesson for you."

My story- How Father taught me to drive after I encountered an accident and crashed his car

I was born in Digboi and brought up in Duliajan; a beautiful, small town in Upper Assam. When I was born, my Father was then working in OIL INDIA LIMITED Duliajan Assam in Drilling Department.

Digboi is also my father's hometown and where he also started working in AOC. So, I was born in his hometown while he was then working for OIL in Duliajan. My Grandfather also worked for AOC. Digboi and Duliajan are sister towns just 30 km apart. Both are oil towns of Assam...

I was fortunate to be brought up in Duliajan town (a township which was built on the imitation of British lifestyle, European fashioned bungalows, clubs, golf courses and a distinctive lifestyle) where we had access to the Zaloni Club. The club had magnificent Lawn Tennis courts, Billiards, TT courts, Swimming pool, Squash, Badminton, etc. During every summer vacation, I used to learn some or the other sport.

I was 14 years old then. One fine day, I told my Father that I wanted to learn car driving. He said ok, and internally, he was very happy that I had the eagerness to learn at such a young age. So, on frequent evenings, when he had to visit the market and also after my tuition, he used to make me sit beside him; on the passenger seat, and teach me how to control the steering of the car and to concentrate on the road. Then we had Fiat Padmini 1987 Model.

It continued for a pretty long time, months passed by and till then I only knew a little about holding and controlling the steering while seated beside him. He never allowed me to sit on the driving seat as he said; we need to go slow & steady. My summer vacation ended, I was really upset and running out of patience. Till now, as I mentioned,

I only knew about the mechanism of the steering wheel to an extent.

In my mind, I harbored the notion that Deuta didn't teach me to drive; am I that worthless? I really wanted to be in the driving seat, change the gears and drive on the road.

One fine Thursday evening, my Mother (she knew driving) and I went to meet Mr. Prakash Chandra Barah (Uncle) and his family. While coming back, I asked my mother to allow me to take the charge of the driving seat. I said to her that I had been taking driving lessons from Father, so she agreed. After the car got in motion, it went beyond my control and in the next moment our car and we were inside the drain nearby. People from the neighboring bungalows, all the servants from the servant quarters, came running and took us out. Thankfully, we were out of harm's way. When I stepped out, I saw I had damaged my uncle's garden, broke their fencing and hedges. It so happened that instead of steering the car out of the gate, I lost control and drove through their garden, bulldozing what stood in the way and landed up in the drain.

The car's front was totally damaged; the radiator was gone, headlights broken, battery smashed, engine dented, number plate destroyed, front tyres gone. Everything was damaged on the front side of the Fiat car. The car was somehow pulled out of the drain with the help of people from the servant quarters. They tied ropes at the back wheel of the car and a few pushed the car from the front side. A crane was called, but the servants had already managed to pull it out before the crane reached. Finally, after it was taken out, we somehow managed to take it back to our then bungalow number F-33.

When the accident happened, my Father came on foot to the spot and saw me standing aside; nervous, quiet and shivering. I thought Father is really going to blast at me.

But when he came near me, he spread his wide arms, hugged me tight and kissed my forehead. The first thing he asked me was, "Have you hurt your back?" I replied no. "Have you got hurt at the back of your head?" I said no. "Are you feeling pain in your chest as the car was inclined vertically?" I said, not that much but a little bit.

I shall never forget what Deuta said that night – "Never mind, it was just a car. I am glad that you failed while trying. I am happy and proud that you have the eagerness to learn. Don t give up. I am there with you." In my whispering and broken voice, I asked, "Father, will I be able to learn driving ever again?" He replied, "You are my daughter, don't give up so easily." He hugged me tight and asked me to sleep without any worry.

Few months after the incident, when his car was already back from the servicing center, I again expressed to Father my wish to learn driving. He said, ok.

One Sunday morning, he took the car out of the garage and called for Raju Kaka (the cook plus the caretaker who worked as the house helper for my Father since his bachelorhood days). Raju Kaka had brought me up like his own daughter, as I was his Sahab's (Sir's) only daughter. Then Father also called Ramesh, who was the gardener. When both of them arrived, Father asked them to give me a bucket (balti) a mug and attach the pipe to the tap. I asked Father, "What are these for and why are you asking them to give me a bucket, mug, pipe, etc.?"

Father smiled and said, "You have to wash the car today. Give emphasis on cleaning the tyres, clean the inside of the car, the floor mats, the steering, etc." I was furious and said to him. "That's not my job. We have the servant staff and also Raju Kaka who can do this."

He replied, "Don't question me, do what I am saying and don't take help from others." After some time, I was seen washing the car, rubbing the floor mats, cleaning the tyres, etc. With a pipe in my hand, a bucket, a mug, my wet clothes, and wet sandals, I almost looked like the other staff in the bungalow. Later, when I was done with the cleaning, Father parked the car back in the garage.

I felt so upset that he made me wash the car in front of everyone... (That was my Ego)

After a few days, Father asked me to change the tyre of the car. Again, I said, "That's not my job." He, again with his composed expressions, said, "Don't question me, do as I say. I was asked to plant the jack near the wheel, turn the lever of the jack, unscrew the bolts of the tyre and change it.

Again after a few days, Father asked me to open the bonnet of the car, clean it, check the mobil oil, brake oil, put water in the radiator. He made me learn how to change the battery; taking out the clamps and fitting it back, pour distilled water into the battery. He taught me how to grease certain parts of the engine with the greasing machine. Then one day, he took me to a local garage near Tipling where he made me watch and learn how the bush parts of the car were changed & how primer painting is done at the bottom to prevent rust. Our Fiat was 87 Padmini model, it was quite different from the kind of cars that roll on the roads today.

After few days, he taught me how to use the dipper, indicator, headlights on the road.

To me, driving was all about sitting on the driver's seat, changing gears and driving on the road. Therefore, I thought that I was only made to do unnecessary things.

On one weekend, Father said, "I am taking the car out of the garage, come and sit on the driving seat, I shall sit beside you. It was like an achievement, I was on top of the world, so happy that from that day onwards that I shall be driving on the roads.

Guess what, for the next few months, I was only made to take out the car of the garage and put it back both ways; forward and backward. He made sure that the tyres were aligned (straight) when I parked the car.

That was like the acid test of my patience, I was angry and had no words to describe. But still, I continued to do whatever Father instructed.

By then, I was of 15 years and my next summer vacation had started. My tuitions for the next session were already on and most of it was in the evening. One evening, after Father fetched me from my tuition, he asked me to sit on the driving seat and he took the seat beside me.

I turned on the ignition of the car, shifted to 1st gear and then the 2nd gear. After going for a few seconds, Father asked me to pull the brakes and stop the car. Then again, I was asked to start the car, and after driving for a few seconds, pull the car to a halt. A fifteen-minute drive from tuition back home took us one hour that day.

A little later that year, I almost knew to drive but my Father always accompanied me as I was below 18 and I didn't have a license.

My Queries to Father

Me: Why did you ask me to wash the car?

Father: Never say it's not your job. Staff who are here may not be there for you tomorrow. Be self-dependent always. (Self-Dependent (Atma Nirbhar) was taught since then.)

Me: Why did you ask me to change the tyre?

Father: What if the tyre gets punctured in the middle of a place where nobody is around. (In those days, there was no on-call servicing.)

Me: Why did you ask me to check all those brake oils, etc.?

Father: It's not only about driving a car on the road; you must also know your car properly; how does it function and what is the importance of all these. You should know your machine before you operate. (Machine, he referred to the car.)

Me: For many days, you only asked me to take the car out of the garage and park it back.

Father: As you are learning, your parking should be perfect and tyers aligned.

Me: Why did you ask to start the car, let me drive for a few seconds and then stop?

Father: It is most important to have control over your mind and brakes. (This will also help you prevent an accident.)

Phew... It was quite a learning at a young age.

He said, "The car falling into the drain was an accident but giving up/not giving up was your choice and you didn't give up. Don't surrender easily in life. Always be alert, look at both sides and drive slow. It shall minimize any kind of uncertain mishappenings."

What Deuta taught – "We learn from failures, not from success. And the most beautiful thing about learning is nobody can take it from you. Once learned, it's all yours. Learn from scratch and chase perfection, excellence. Always strive for continuous improvement. Be patient..."

Chapter Five

Bed Time Stories

Father narrated an incident that dates back to somewhere around more than half a century ago, during his bachelor days in OIL.

It was in the late 60s or early 70s when he was posted in one of the oil well sites at a remote place in Upper Assam. What he told me was, there was dense forest, and they were at one of the well sites for Oil Drilling.

There was a base camp and he was in charge of the project.

Back then, most of the Oil Drilling work was done manually. So there were several gang men and other juniors who were working under him.

One late evening, one worker came to his personal camp and here's the communication that followed:

Father: Ki hol kele kam rokhile (What happened, why has the work stopped)?

Gang man: Saaaar, (that's how village people pronounce Sir) ami tate kam nokoru (We will not work here).

Father: Why??

Gang man: Aye tate pipe bohabole khandithakute konkal pale (While we are digging the mud to lay the pipe, we found a human skeleton). Aru tate bhoot ase (and there are ghosts).

Father: Let's go together, check the human skeleton and find the ghost.

Upon reaching the spot, Father asked another gang man to dig a grave at another place near the tree which was nearby. He took the skeleton from the site's location and laid him/her in peace in his/her new place with his own hands. He also lit an earthen lamp and some incense sticks near the remains and buried him/her.

And about the ghost story, Father said to the laborers/ gang men not to be afraid because the ghost was afraid of him. In short, he manipulated the fear and belief of the innocent laborers that if they tell the ghost that they are working with Father, the ghost will get scared and run away. He stayed awake all night with them so that work was not hampered and of course, to give the courage to the laborers and keep them away from ghost stories.

I remember the same strategy Father applied on me when I was a kid.

This was after watching the Bollywood horror movie Veerana, I could not sleep for several nights. One night, he asked me to say this before sleeping… I am my Father's daughter, nothing can scare me. And believe me, it worked. He manipulated my belief too that if I say that I am his daughter, the ghost/fear will vanish.

He later revealed that such affirmations were a hack to rewire the belief system and let go of the fears.

I think it was not only the trick of taking his name but also his heroic and tough presence with his big mustache and masculine body. He almost looked like an Army officer (as also mentioned by a Former Oil Indian in his tribute). He was my Hero.

There was a time when he was also nicked named as the Royal Bengal Tiger of Duliajan and Digboi by his loved ones at his workplace for his tough and strong appearance.

So even now when I feel scared, I just say this in my mind: **I am my Father's Daughter.**

He had numerous ways to encourage me—

If I said, "I am scared," he would reply while rolling his mustache, "Ek sher ka beti hoke tum ghabrata hain?" (Being a tiger's daughter, you feel scared?) With these affirmations imbibed within me since childhood, I fight every disappointment in life with courage and endure a mind without fear.

Me: *Deuta why did you dig another place and buried the skeleton again?*

Deuta: (I was around 7 or 8 then) The death rituals vary according to different religions. For example, we are Hindus, when we die, our body is cremated, then the ashes are submerged in a flowing river or sea; it dissolves with the nature. This completes the journey back to God's home.

However, in some religions, the body is buried. The journey ends when it fully dissolves into the earth.

So, for our work, we had to dig him/her out and bury at a different place so that he/she can complete the journey to God's home. I just helped him/her to complete the journey (which was disrupted by us for work) to reach the ultimate destination.

I was never taught of hell or heaven. Whatever you do; good or bad, your karma will make you live through it in this birth. This is what Father taught.

He was a very emotional man.

Another such story is also related to their Oil Drilling camp based in the dense place of Upper Assam. This is too a late 60s or 70s incident.

(I precisely can't recall which well site and which location it was. In case someone who is from AOC or OIL, who knows it elaborately, may write to the email given at the back of the book. It shall be updated in the next edition.)

This is what Father narrated and what I can recall.

Father and team were based on a very interior place for their Oil Drilling Project with a huge dense forest around.

One day, while returning to their camp from the well site, the vehicle in which Father and 4/5 of his crew members got stuck in the middle of an elevated slope. There was a broken patch on the road amidst the dense forest. The tyres of the vehicle sunk into the red mud. The more the driver tried to press the throttle, the more the spinning tyres dug into the mud. At that moment, the only option they could think of was to pull the vehicle out through ropes. As they were making the preparation, it started to drizzle.

It often rains heavily in those areas, so the driver must be skilled enough to deal with such roads and travel. Suddenly, the thunder burst and it started raining so heavily that the water was flowing at a high speed towards the vehicle. The vehicle was stuck and nobody was able to move. It was pouring so heavily that the water started clogging in the vehicle in no time. All of them were highly strung by the situation.

Deuta was known for his skill in lifting heavy tools as many things were done manually in the well sites. (Also, there is a humorous bachelorhood story of him shared by both; Uncle Ajit Mahanta and Uncle Manas Bordoloi in the tributes section, wherein Father along with his friend lifted a car)

So when they were in a tight spot in the vehicle, Deuta, sensing the gravity of the situation, got down from the car in almost waist-deep water. In that torrent of rain, he, with his strong hands and all his strength, pushed the car to a point where the rest of the crew members could get out of the vehicle and find shelter. Each crew member was pulled out from the vehicle by Deuta. Then the driver managed to drive the vehicle to a safer place. That was how they managed to survive a really tough day.

There are scores of stories from wild animals chasing them, especially wild elephants, to flooding and drilling under severe conditions in the remote areas of Upper Assam, Arunachal Pradesh and many other places. Deuta always had to carry a shotgun to shoo away the wild animals. At that time, few of them, including Deuta were also very fond of hunting.

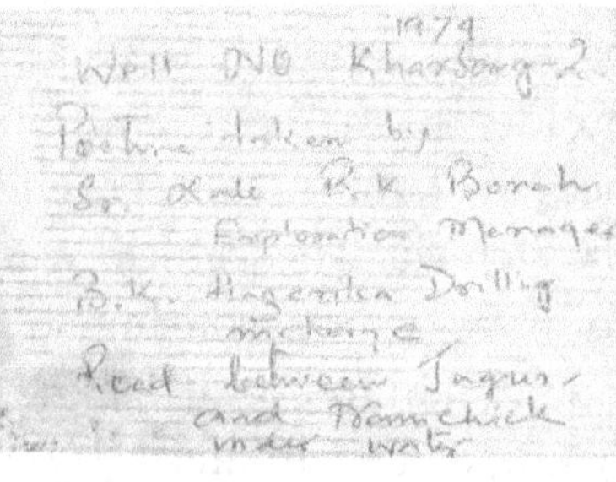

Father (Drilling In-charge) **(Road between Jagur and Namchick underwater)** on the way to well number Kharsang 2 in 1974 on an elephant in a flood-affected time.

This picture was taken by Late R.K Borah, Exploration Manager Of B.K.Hazarika.

Father believed in a famous quote from Bhagawat Gita "No one should abandon duties because he sees defects in them. Every action, every activity is surrounded by defects as fire is surrounded by smoke."

Chapter Six

Surprise Test Failed

I recall an incident; I was in grade 9th. I was a student of Kendriya Vidyalaya Duliajan for most of my life (before that; I studied in St. Joesph High School Bhubaneswar and St. Xaviers School Duliajan). It so happened that one day, our Geography teacher entered the class and said, "I have a surprise test for you students." Generally, besides half-yearly and final exams, we had unit tests every month and the dates of the tests were shared beforehand. So needless to say, I used to mug up and appear for the test. But the surprise test was something that took the entire class by surprise except one or two students. We were given a blank map of the world and we had to identify the places. Apart from one or two students, the entire class, including me, failed. Those who failed were asked to stand outside the class for the next couple of hours. Before leaving the class, the teacher categorically asked to get the test copy signed by our respective Fathers. Now that was the toughest part we had to face after going home.

I went home and with great courage, informed Father about the marks I had got. Rolling his mustache, he said, "You have got very less marks. It took me barely 5 mins to solve the paper. Geography is a wonderful subject." Without reacting too much, he signed the test copy. He, of course, asked me what went wrong. I said it was a surprise test, and I was not prepared for it. I added that the subject was turning out to be too difficult for me.

Back then, like many teenagers, I had a huge crush on the Hollywood actor, Tom Cruise. So, my room was filled with all Tom Cruise posters from Cocktail to Top Gun, name it and I had the poster. One poster was on the bedside, the other was pasted in front of the study table, one poster was at the door, and so on.

A couple of days later, Father got some huge posters printed from his office and some he bought from the market. My entire Tom Cruise posters, especially the one in front of my study table, were replaced by World Maps. So instead of staring at the posters of Tom Cruise, every morning, I had to ogle at the Maps and that was quite disheartening at that point in time as a teenager.

My homework was to just glare at the maps for 10 minutes after waking up.

What he taught me was, never mug up, just let your subconscious mind fell in love with the subject. It's a practice and you must do it to overcome your weakness.

He was aware of my crush, so he said to me, "You can paste him (Tom Cruise) back when your exams are over." I did fell in love with the subject and that was how I managed to score well in my 12th grade.

HE BELIEVED IN THE FAMOUS QUOTE OF BRIAN HERBERT- "THE CAPACITY TO LEARN IS A GIFT; THE ABILITY TO LEARN IS A SKILL, THE WILLINGNESS TO LEARN IS A CHOICE."

Chapter Seven

Love for Pets

A long time back, in his bachelorhood days, Deuta had two mix-breed dogs. One named Bhim and the other named Dara. They both were taken care of mainly by Raju Kaka (as mentioned earlier, he was the caretaker plus the cook for a very long time).

Father loved his dogs from the bottom of his heart. He often told stories about how they both used to wait for Father to come from his work. The mutts refused to eat their meals if not served by my Father. But it was not always possible for Father as he had long working hours. But whenever he was at home, he made sure that he spent maximum time with Bhim and Dara

A few years later, Bhim died of some illness. Dara was an emotional pet, he too died later.

Father never adopted any pets after that because he was heartbroken as he mentioned.

Years later, I was born and it was when we shifted back from Bhubaneswar to Duliajan in the year 1987.

One fine morning, there was one little stray dog puppy who found her way to our then bungalow premises, she was probably a month old. We named her Kili.

Deuta made a wooden house for her, which he placed in the back verandah (balcony) of our house. Kili was very lovingly taken care of.

When she grew up, she used to very eagerly wait for Father to come back from the office.

As soon as she saw his car at the gate, she used to welcome him excitedly, with all her love.

After a few years, we came to know she was pregnant.

If we had these digital cameras at that time, I would have certainly clicked the moment when it was a very cold night in December, Deuta was sitting in front of the fireplace in the living room and pregnant Kili was taking a nap beside him. I have very fond memories of Father's unexplainable bond and love with Kili.

She later delivered 7 puppies in our premises.

There was a time when our bungalow number F-33 in Duliajan Oil Town, besides being a home to humans, was also a shelter to 12 stray dogs, one pet cat (who was there with us for close to 8 yrs.), few more visiting cats, many chickens, and frequent visitors both (poisonous & non-poisonous) like snakes and birds.

The staff of the bungalow was often seen shooing away the reptile and bird visitors.

The heart-warming memory I could recall is when they (the pet dogs, cat Meenu) all used to rush towards the car as soon as Deuta arrived.

Love unconditionally; that's what Father taught.

> *"A joyful heart emanates from unconditional love."*
> — Late Bimal Kumar Hazarika

Chapter Eight

Be Spiritually Connected

F ather was a devotee of Lord Shiva.

I recall, every evening, after coming from the office, he used to chant Lord Shiva Mantra, and took a bath before his dinner.

He usually took us to the now Tilinga Shiva Mandir which is in Tinsukia district Bordubi Assam, near Duliajan Oil Town. It was a must-visit for us on every Shivratri, before the crack of the dawn. Back then, there was a big Banyan Tree in the middle of a tea garden, under which Shiva Linga was found. So, I remember, we used to visit that tea garden, treading our way to the holy tree and offering prayers. I have cherished memories of those times when we visited during Shivratri, we could see people chanting Lord Shiva mantras late at night, sitting under that tree.

The history of this temple dates back to more than half a decade when the tea garden workers found a black rock, in the shape of Shiva Lingam, emerging from the ground under the Banyan Tree. It was unearthed and nestled around the roots of the tree. Over the years, people have discovered its mysterious power: make a wish and it will be granted.

Now it has been developed into a big Shiva Temple; Tilinga (which means bell in Assamese). People hang a bell (Tilinga) on the branches of the tree and pray for their wishes to come true.

Even today, one of the fondest memories is visiting the Temple with my Late Father.

Om Namah Shivay

Chapter Nine

His Teachings

- He always taught life will never be an easy path, so develop the ability to work tirelessly towards a goal. Most of all, be a source of endless energy, be motivated to win, and be the best in whatever you are doing.

- Love Unconditionally.

- Be spiritually connected.

- Don't stop learning. Keep growing. Keep studying. Keep exploring yourself. Always harbor a learner's attitude. (He read enormous books on his profession Crude Oil Drilling, world history, geography, different languages (I still have one of his books on learning Spanish and mathematics).

- He always taught and believed in a famous quote by Mahatma Gandhi- "LIVE AS IF YOU WERE TO DIE TOMORROW. LEARN AS IF YOU WERE TO LIVE FOREVER."

- Just believe in yourself be patient.

- Failure must never be a reason to quit. Keep trying.

- It's not important how many times you have failed, but you must get up and keep going till you win.

- Spend wisely and develop a habit of saving.

- Aim high and put your heart into whatever you do in your life.

Dear Father (Deuta)

I have always missed you.

Love

Daughter (Apunar ek matra Borkanya) (Your only daughter)

This reminds me of a quote from Bhagwat Gita that I firmly believe in - *"The Individual soul is infrangible and insoluble, and can neither be burned or destroyed. He is everlasting, present everywhere, unchangeable, immovable and internally the same."*

Chapter Ten

Tributes by Former OIL Indian in
their own words

Tribute by Mr. Abani Barua
Former OIL Indian
OIL INDIA LIMITED

I remember Bimalda as a man of iron resolve with a very soft heart. A man of unquestionable professional honesty and integrity.

After joining the Company (OIL) in the year 1973, I had a long association with Bimalda, a very strict taskmaster who had just returned from an overseas training stint in the North Seas. Our batch of 5 Drilling engineers learned our trade the hard way. Bimalda made us serve and assemble various drilling equipment with our own hands. I still remember his philosophy, "There are no shortcuts to on-the-hand job experience, and hard work."

Let me recollect one of my memorable experiences when working under Bimal Da. Bimalda had just tied the knot with Arly Bou. I was in the well site (9 to 5 night slot) at a remote location. Late at night or early morning, there were some problems at the site and very reluctantly, I had to inform Bimalda, who instructed to check certain mud (drilling fluid) parameter and give him further feedback. (Normally you do not disturb any DIC in this odd hour.) I asked the mud attendant to recheck the mud parameter and report back. Meanwhile, the problem continued. I had to report back that everything looked okay, but the problem persisted (heavy backflow during pulling out the drill string). Bimalda promptly asked me to stop everything and continue circulation. Shortly afterward, in about half an hour's time, I saw Bimalda getting down from his car (no driver) and reached the derrick floor. He then rushed to the chemical attendant's shed, rechecked the mud himself, and found a huge abnormality. He did not scold me but told me firmly that in any such event do not depend on others but verify personally. That was a lesson that I can never forget that such laxity leads to drilling catastrophe.

I also had the experience of working under Bimalda at the Bay Exploration Project, Bhubaneswar, when OIL did their second venture for offshore oil exploration in the Bay of Bengal. It was hard work at the office, which continued till late evening and very often ended with an enjoyable dinner at his home prepared by our dear Arly Bou. I was a bachelor then, and I remember Bimalda's family taking me on trips to the marketplace for ice cream and dosas at Venus Inn!

Life was fun and work was challenging, being new to the offshore environment.

– Abani Barua

Tribute by
Mr. Sidharth Deb
Former OIL Indian
OIL INDIA LIMITED

It was a sultry June morning in Duliajan. The year was 1968. Four young men, fresh out of engineering colleges, waited anxiously in a completely strange environment. They were about to embark upon a career with Oil India Limited (OIL). The young men were Manoj Sharma, Tarjeet Singh, Balasubramaniam (Bala) and me; - Siddhartha Deb. Tarjeet and I were local lads having grown up in Digboi, a sister town about 35 km away.

It was a busy morning at the drilling department. The hectic activities around made us a bit nervous. The office where we all waited was manned by a dignified elderly gentleman who appeared to be perpetually on the phone. Half an hour earlier, he waived us to a few wooden chairs and told us to wait; - a senior executive of the department, our designated trainer would be here soon.

A car screeched to a stop. It was a black Ambassador. A man with a mustache and a gait resembling a senior army officer walked in. We were soon introduced to him. He was Mr. Bimal Kumar Hazarika, the gentleman we were eagerly waiting for. We were a bit tense at his rough and tough exterior, but a bright smile and warm handshakes put us at ease. Within a couple of days, he became our Bimal-da, a friend, philosopher, guide and mentor till my last day at OIL. He was not really a stranger to me. Being a Digboi resident, I knew his family. One of his brothers was my contemporary at schools, probably a year younger.

Early morning the next day, a vehicle came to our mess to transport us to the drilling rig. He was already at the site and working when we arrived. He looked a little grim as we stood in front of him for instructions. There was no trace of a smile on his face as he passed on his first instruction. He ordered us to get some cleaning oil and cotton waste and clean the threads of the huge number of pipes piled on a rack on site. We were stunned. We were engineers, - cleaning pipes was not our job!

Well, we had no choice. We stood under the scorching sun and got on with the job. A few hours later, a member of the crew came and said "sahib" was calling us. We reached the small portable office at the site. This time, he greeted us with a big smile and asked whether we enjoyed our assignment. We stood still. He looked at us and burst out in loud laughter and said, - "Tomorrow's assignment will be tougher and dirtier. Next few months, you all will work as members of the crew and learn their jobs before you step into my shoes. You know why? Because this activity will teach you the dignity of labor and the pain and agony of the crew members who will be working under you."

These words were prophetic. This was an advice I carried with me till the last day of my career. We need to feel the pain, agony and emotions of the people working for us.

Our contact with Bimalda was restricted to our interactions at the drill site. He was a very popular personality. People welcomed him cheerfully whenever he walked into a get-together, a party or the club bar, which he frequented quite often. One evening, a few of my friends and I decided to call on him for a social visit. We were a bit hesitant as we pressed the doorbell. The front door was wide open. Duliajan was a quiet, peaceful and secure town where safety was never under threat and nobody bolted the front door. Seconds later, a young domestic helper came and opened the door. His name was Raju. If someday I write a biography of Bimalda, at least a chapter will be dedicated to Raju. He was Bimalda's Man-Friday, taking care of all his household work including shopping, cooking, cleaning, etc. Raju ushered us into the living room. The place looked like a typical bachelor's pad. Soon Bimalda joined us. He was so happy to see us that he gave all of us a bear-hug. Tea and snacks were served and suddenly he announced, - "You guys will stay back and have dinner with me." Our spontaneous protests were spurned away with a wave of his strong hand. Raju looked confused, disturbed and mumbled something illegible. It was obvious he was not prepared to cater to four extra heads. Bimalda stretched out; reached and picked up something which looked like a wallet lying carelessly in one corner of a side table. He pulled out a sheaf of notes and handed them over to Raju without counting. This was another aspect of his personality; Bimalda was totally indifferent about money. He was generous to the core; anyone seeking his help was never disappointed. There are several instances of people taking undue advantage of his generosity. To cut a long story short, it was a lovely dinner with lavish servings of mutton curry, which was literally our host's staple item at dinner, every night without fail!

Personally, I came very close to him a few years later, when I was transferred to Moran for a drilling project headed by him. Among the drillers, I was the youngest, a bachelor and with the least experience. I was told that Bimalda personally handpicked me. This boosted my morale immensely. This was a stage of my career when I matured greatly as a professional. His dedication, hard work, loyalty and integrity left a deep impression on me. People of that generation took their work as worship or sacred duty, a trait which is on the wane these days. He was always in competition, with himself. He was passionately involved in breaking his own records, - and there were several.

The last time I worked with him was in Arunachal Pradesh on a project at Manabhum. The camp life in the dense forest under his leadership was fascinating. In 1980, I received an offer from Kuwait Oil Company. I visited Bimalda to break the news. He was married by then and so was I. If he was disappointed at my impending resignation; he did not show it and congratulated me wholeheartedly and wished me the best. We promised to stay in touch. There was no internet or e-mails in those days; even international phone calls were flawed. He was not the letter-writing type. But I always bore in mind a deep desire to return and meet with him. That never happened. The devastating news of his premature departure from this world reached me and I went under a spell of depression.

I am sure he is as happy and jovial in the other world as well as he has always been.

Miss you Bimalda.

– Sidharth Deb

Tribute by

Mr. Biren Das

Former OIL Indian

OIL INDIA LIMITED

Remembering Bimalda…

When we were young engineers, working in Oil India Limited, the name of Shri Bimal Hazarika (Bimalda) was uttered in great respect, awe and love. His presence always radiated confidence and joy in a group, whether it was in the well site or a get-together party or the official meetings.

His gentle demeanor was in sharp contrast to the rough and tough nature of activities in the drilling department that he was leading. That fills us with awe. He addressed us with great love and never let us feel small against his vast knowledge and experience and being a towering figure in the company. Today I remember dear Bimalda with my pranaams to him.

Also, my pranaams to dear Bimalda Bou with whom I had some memorable moments, one of them being a table tennis partner with her in doubles competition in Zaloni Club when we won the championship.

Those were the golden days of our life.

– *Biren Das*

Tribute by
Mr. Swadhin Hazarika
Former OIL Indian
Oil India Limited

Whenever I think about Bimalda (Late Bimal Kumar Hazarika), I can feel his profound love and affection for me. He loved me as his own brother. As far as I remember, I first met Bimalda in the interview that was held on completion of 6 months of my 2-year Graduate Engineer Training program in Oil India Limited. He happened to be one of the members of the interview board. During the interview, Mr. Padmapati of the Administrative department wanted to know my feelings and observations about being in OIL. I said that in general I had enjoyed working in OIL. However, I added that I found the approach of some senior officers somewhat cold and indifferent. At this, Mr. Padmapati sarcastically (as perceived by me at that time) commented that probably these officers didn't like me. I gently opined about the remote possibility of his view, stating that almost all my friends who had joined OIL in our batch had the same opinion as mine about the dealings of some of the senior officials of the company towards us. For a few moments, there was silence in the interview room. Then Bimalda started speaking in his deep voice. First, he asked a few technical questions. He then wanted to know about my family and my interest in games and sports. At last, he looked at me straight in the eyes and assured me that from that day onward, I should not worry about anything. He advised me to work hard, go about learning my job and freely participate in games and other activities of Zaloni Club. He assured me that no senior official would be ever cold and indifferent towards me and my friends. I didn't expect this and was overwhelmed by those soothing and encouraging words. At that moment, he truly won me and my trust. What happened the next day evening in the Zaloni Club was a pleasant surprise. When I entered the Zaloni Club bar, one senior executive present there warmly greeted me in a friendly manner and enquired about my tennis, and how I was doing. I was further taken aback when he offered me a drink. I could realize later on that this was all due to Bimalda's benign initiative. The deep bond of love, trust and goodwill between me and Bimalda strengthened over the years, with me as the privileged beneficiary.

A few months after joining OIL in 1973, I was transferred to Kharsang well no. 2 in the Tirap district of Arunachal Pradesh to work as an Assistant to Rig Engineer Mr. P. K. Sikdar. I was there in the Kharsang well site camp for about a year, starting from rig movement through drilling operations. I was fortunate to find Bimalda as the Drilling-in-charge of the well. My learning of rig engineering and enriching personal relationships with Bimalda started in Kharsang under his caring and watchful eyes. At this point in time, I remember another distinguished personality with love and great respect. He was Late Ranjit Kumar Barua (Senior), who at that time was the Exploration Superintendent of the Ningru area and was stationed in the Kharsang camp. I considered myself blessed in the company of these two unique personalities. The care, guidance and unstinted

support of these two great souls at an early stage of my professional career immensely contributed to my technical and personal development. My days in the well site camp amid the deep jungle at the foothills of Patkai range were full of adventure, thrill and challenges. I get nostalgic when I remember a few occasions of midnight hunting expeditions I took part in with these two Dadas (Brothers) during some lean period of well site activities. I was responsible for the maintenance of batteries of the well site and at their advice on a particular night, I would load two 12 Volt heavy-duty batteries onto the back of an open jeep along with a maneuverable searchlight connected to the batteries. Usually, Bimalda would be behind the steering wheel and Late Barua would be sitting beside him with his loaded American carbine. Needless to say that Bimalda's shotgun would also be lying within easy reach by his side. My role was to stand or perch on the bench seat at the rear of the open jeep and throw the searchlight beam on the roadside jungle to spot a prey, be it deer, boar or any other wild animal. Though these few hunting trips didn't yield any success for the duo in terms of a prize, these were great moments of real living for me. After returning from the hunt, I would go to bed at around 3 AM only and hence couldn't attend office timely the next morning. However, both the main hunters were present in their respective offices right on time. On one such occasion, Mr. Sikdar gently reproached me, the assistant hunter (☺), for being such a sleepyhead!

There's another incident that showed the kind of person Bimalda was. I was the Mess Manager of Kharsang Camp for some time when I was wholeheartedly assisted by Mr. Swaran Singh, the Senior Electrical Engineer. I was on a weekly marketing trip to Jagun in a truck on a rainy summer evening. On our way back from the market, after a few hours, we were informed at Namchik Gate that a stretch of the road towards the campsite had been washed away by the flash flood. At that time, it was raining cats and dogs. When the intensity of the rain didn't recede till about midnight, we decided to take a chance and proceeded to the camp. Our vehicle was a high-bed, company-owned Tata truck. When we reached the breach portion, I was shocked to see in the headlight of the truck that there was no road and, in its place, a rapid foamy river was flowing across the road. In consultation with the driver, we decided to ford the 70/80 feet stretch. Several times, the headlights came under the surface of the rushing flood water and momentarily, we were left in total darkness. I had to lean out through the truck window and use a powerful torch light to illuminate the water path. I feared that at any moment our vehicle would be washed away into the deep roadside jungle. However, thanks to our driver, we could cross the treacherous and violent water body due to his sheer grit and expertise. When we finally reached the camp, everyone was asleep except Bimalda. The door of his troco house was ajar, and I found him sitting on a sofa with a drink in front of him, his shotgun near him leaning against the sofa back. He looked deeply concerned and was visibly relieved to see me. I was all soaked in rainwater, and he offered me a drink. He said that in another 15 minutes, he would have gone out in search of me. I lack the vocabulary to express my feelings at that moment. This was Bimalda, all empathy and compassion; and I was deeply moved.

For me, Bimalda was a symbol of extraordinary physical strength, courage and determination. Like many of his colleagues from erstwhile AOC, work meant worship for him. I had tremendous admiration for his never-say-die attitude. His very presence radiated confidence and enthusiasm. He encouraged us to work hand in hand with the work persons. He asserted that the hands-on experience would enhance learning about the plants and equipment and boost our confidence. During my time as a workover engineer, I remember one incident when I tried to be extra-heroic and emulate Bimalda's feat. We were transferring Static equipment of workover operation from a production well near Madhapur Tiniali to another location. I, with the help of a group of employees, was loading a few 6» Gate valves with short flanged nipples onto the back side of a low-bed company-owned Bedford van. When I noticed two tradesmen struggling to lift one such valve assembly onto the van, I approached the twosome. I advised them to step aside, lifted the assembly off the ground with all my strength and put it in the van. While doing this, I felt a creaking in my lower back, near the tailbone. After returning to the office, I felt discomfort in my lower back and the next day, consulted Dr. Kumar in OIL Hospital. After a thorough check-up, Dr. Kumar advised proper rest for a week and strongly advised against driving a motorbike and playing tennis. I was also playfully reprimanded for my unwise action at the well site. From that incident, I understood very clearly that I was a long way from matching Bimalda's prowess.

I had the unique privilege of enjoying the kind hospitality of Bimalda and Arly Bou in terms of the innumerable lunch, dinner and other meals they lovingly shared with me, mostly during my bachelor days. After about a month of our marriage, I, as Rig Engineer, had to attend a late-night cementing job in a drilling well in the Joypur area near Nahorkotia. Bimalda was the Drilling-In- Charge of the well. As my wife Raj would be all alone at home, I took her along with me to the well site in my old Hindustan 14 car. The next day, Bimalda came to know that Raj was at the well site sitting inside a car throughout the previous night. He felt so miserable that he made me promise that in such situations in the future, I should leave Raj in Arly Bou's care in their house. This was Bimalda with the golden heart.

May the noble soul of Bimalda always find a place in the Almighty's divine embrace!

– Swadhin Hazarika

Tribute by
Mr. Santikam Hazarika
Former OIL Indian
OIL INDIA LIMITED

I still remember my first encounter with Bimal Hazarika. Nearly half a century ago, I had just joined OIL at Duliajan, and as part of my induction, my first field trip was to a drilling well site. The well was located in the midst of the dense Jorajan forest. In the driller's hut, I came across a figure with a strikingly ferocious handlebar, whose personality seemed to be exercising a mesmerising control over everyone present in the well site by his mere presence. I approached him with a degree of trepidation, but very soon, the veneer crust seemed to have fallen off and I found that the tough exterior actually harboured a dainty heart, full of compassion. Like many others, I soon became a fan of his.

The senior Drillers in those days were a separate breed in OIL, a spectacularly diverse lot, most of them toughened by their Burmah Oil background exploring for the elusive liquid gold a few kilometres below the ebullient terrains of Upper Assam. And amidst this maverick lot, Bimal Hazarika managed to carve a niche for himself through his deft technical and personnel skills. After failing in their initial efforts, in the early 1970s, OIL decided to re-explore for OIL in the undulating terrains of Kharsang in Arunachal Pradesh with greater determination and preparation. Who else but Bimal Hazarika was chosen as the Driller in Charge to pilot the whole adventure, fraught with uncertainty. And lo, very soon, Arunachal Pradesh got added to the oil map of India.

Most Duliajanites, as bachelors, would remember Bimalda, often walking into the Zaloni Club Bar just a few minutes before Bar Closing. Normally at that time, there would only be a few bachelors at the bar, bored beyond belief. Bimalda would order "one for the road" for all the stragglers and a *gup shup* session would put life back into them.

Again, when OIL ventured into the uncertain waters off the Orissa Coast, Bimalda was sent as the Drilling Head, an obvious choice. For all visitors, his abode in Bhubaneswar was more important than the customary darshan of Lord Jagannath and yours truly also availed his legendary hospitality with Sangita and Ronku, who was a mere toddler at that time.

Later on, I had the opportunity to work closely with him when I was transferred to Bhubaneswar. I was truly impressed by his incisiveness, being able to go deep into details and read beyond the lines of the complex technical specifications of the equipment being handled in offshore drilling, a very different cup of tea from what was being dealt with at the Nahorkatiya and Moran fields. No one could take him for granted. He was what it requires to be a true professional.

He faced life as it came, never complained. When I met him the last time in Guwahati, after he became aware of the impending inevitable, he was stoically philosophical about it and I was deeply moved. He was indeed a rare human being.

– Shantikam Hazarika

Tribute by
Mr. Puna Borgohain.
Former OIL Indian
Oil India Limited

As I remember Bimal da...

To me, it's a little odd to say 'Bimal da' as I had known Late Bimal Kumar Hazarika as Putul Kokaiedo since my childhood, i.e. probably from 1961.

Putul Kokaiedo, son of Late Badan Chandra Hazarika, was very close to our family members, i.e. Bordewta, Borma, Dewta, Aie (Ma) Peha, Pehi, Khura, Khuri. This was due to Bordewta's close friendship with Late Badan Chandra Hazarika. Kokaiedo called Bordewta Towiti (Father's friend).

Because of this relationship, Putul Kokaiedo continued to be our family friend and remembered by one and all. Sometimes, he used to be a terror but mostly, the most loving and dear person of all our dear people, irrespective of his age. The relationship between the families developed as my Bordewta worked in AOC Digboi.

His visit to our ancestral home, Sibsagar, is always remembered by one and all at home.

I had some disconnection with Kokaiedo during my study days in school and engineering college

After passing out of college, I joined Oil India Limited in 1976 (May) in Drilling Department.

Here, I again came across Putul Kokaiedo who was now known as Bimalda.

Bimalda, a legend in the Drilling Department in Oil India Limited, his unfailable dedication to his duty was his hallmark.

I shall however, not embark on this familiar subject but concisely narrate my experience of Bimalda's camp life at "Deohal Drilling Camp".

We were about eight trainees who were put in training in a Drilling Well at Deohal (near Tingri) in the morning shift from 5 am to 1 pm under the guidance of Bimalda. We were camping at the well site drilling camp (meant for key personal only). This all happened in 1976.

There, we came to know Bimalda was newly married (which probably was a late marriage) to our dear Arly Bou.

We came to know that the newly married couple was in the camp; a privilege only Bimalda got, as married couples were not allowed in the camp in those days.

We interacted with Bimalda and Bou whenever opportunity permitted; during tea or lunch break or for a talk as boss.

Bimalda never hesitated to show his affection to Bou, which she accepted with a shy smile.

It was a really wonderful experience to see the newly married couple blossoming their affection without any reservation. We will always remember those moments of camp life of Bimalda as a most affectionate Husband.

Those were the moments to be seen to believe, but I have vivid memories and wish life is always like that.

Later, we had moved on in life with many stories in life and work, but we had to meet somewhere again.

I was posted in BVEP (Brahmaputra Valley Exploration Project) in1995.

I was staying in Bamunimaidan Flat in 1997.

Bimalda was also living in a flat in the same building, apparently during Bimalda's illness.

We happened to be of some help during the last days of his journey. We were fortunate to be there in the difficult times faced by all the family members

Life is sometimes lovely, even though the whole world seems to be very busy around you.

– Puna Borgohain

Tribute by
Mr. Manasjyoti Bordoloi
Former OIL Indian
OIL INDIA LIMITED

Bimalda continues to live in our minds…

Whenever I think of Bimalda or recall his association with us in our young days in OIL, he literally comes alive in my mind. Although he is gone a long time back, but my memory of him is refreshingly fresh and his image appears in my mind as a live person. He was a unique person, and he made an indelible impression on our young minds. Bimalda had an aura of invincibility about him and we were regaled with many tales of his almost superhuman physical ability. One such tale is about Bimalda and Rohiteswar Saikiada, another stalwart of OIL in those days, together lifting an Ambassador car and placing it crosswise in the garage of the owner at night. The owner of the car, poor fellow, was at a loss of how to take the car out of the garage. He, of course, rightly concluded that no ordinary mortal could do this feat, and the super-strong duo must be the ones pulling off this prank. He promptly signed off a bar chit for one crate of beer, as demanded by the heroes, and got that owner's car lifted back to its normal parking position!

Bimalda was full of fun but was also dead serious about his work. I had the good fortune to work under him in the drilling of exploration wells at Kharsang and Kumchai (Arunachal Pradesh). Those days (early to late seventies) drilling technology was primitive by today's standard and drilling a deep exploration well was a challenging task mentally and physically. The DIC (Drilling in charge) was literally all in all and the position demanded leadership qualities like team building capability, ability to take the risk, and most importantly, willingness to take responsibility for the entire team across various departments. Bimalda fitted the bill for this challenging position, and we all felt secure working with him. We were inspired to give our best.

In those days, Bimalda, with his core group of geologists, chemists, etc. used to stay in the drilling well site camp at Kumchai, which was right beside the drilling well. So all the time, he was aware of what was going on in the well. He was so devoted to the job that he refused to take his due break from duty if he foresaw some problem in the well. And sometimes he would continue for many weeks without taking a break. On one such occasion, I remember Bimalda showing us with a mischievous smile on his face, the radio message from Arli Bou (they were a newly married couple at that time) demanding that he should come home immediately!!

While Bimalda, with his core group of experts, stayed at the Kumchai well camp, we stayed at the Manabhum base camp, which was about an hour's drive from the well camp. One evening I received a 3-star radio message from DIC that myself and Anjan Kotoky must urgently come to the well site to rectify the defect in the electrical system of the BOP (Blow out preventer). A 3-star message and that too for a problem in the BOP system – you gotta run boy! When we reached the well camp after one hour of Jeep drive in the dusty road, we saw the place buzzing with spirited activity in the brightly lit front side of the camp. And there was also a badminton game going on. And Bimalda was majestically sitting by the courtside, enjoying the game. There was no hint of a serious problem at the well site. With a mischievous smile on his face, Bimalda welcomed us warmly and asked us to first help ourselves to the snacks and local wine that was laid out at a table. After we had our fill, Bimalda explained to us the purpose of the 3-star urgent message – he wanted me and Anjan to come and participate in the badminton competition that was organized that evening at the camp. And the sure-shot way to get us there was faking an urgent situation at the well!! Needless to say, we felt privileged and enjoyed ourselves thoroughly – food, wine and a game of badminton. That was Bimalda – making life interesting, even in a remote and difficult place like Kumchai.

Bimalda was very fond of me and Anjan, but he was wary of us two going out together outside of the camp. Once in a while, we would go out to places like Digboi and Margherita for buying some essential goods for the Manabhum camp mess. While returning, we sometimes visited club bars in the region and have a drink or two in a 5-star ambience. We used to look forward to these trips. When we seek permission for such trips, Bimalda would ask if it is necessary for both of us to go. We managed to find good enough reasons or was it Bimalda's kindness towards us) and he invariably relented. One day, he told us the reason: you two are very dependable individually but when you go out together, I worry what kind of mischief you will be up to!! We, of course, never landed into serious trouble in those trips but once in a while, we would be tempted to take those extra pegs at the bar and arrive quite late at the camp which was what worried Bimalda.

The above is a glimpse of the camp life we lived in a remote place like Manabhum and Kumchai where the challenge of drilling a deep exploration was huge and living conditions were barely comfortable. But difficult conditions made life more interesting because we had somebody like Bimalda to take care of us at work and also beyond work. He was full of zest at work and beyond. The relationship we built, continued throughout our life. This relationship is built on love and trust. I realize now that has been possible because Bimalda, in his heart of hearts, was a very kind person which showed through and touched us deeply.

And thank you Binita for letting me be a part of your wonderful venture.

– Manasjyoti Bordoloi

Tribute by

Mr. Ajit Mahanta

Former OIL Indian

OIL INDIA LIMITED

Machos with Golden hearts...!!

I t was in OIL Setup at Moran many many years back...

A couple arranged a lovely dinner with chosen drinks, music and above all, foods with spreading aroma to the neighboring bungalows...

The party went off very, very well...the guest couples joked, giggled enjoyed themselves...the last-minute thanking and saying 'good night' near the gate with laughters went on for quite some time... the noise of joys filled the area across few bungalows...!

Mr. Chand and his wife, the host of the party, were very happy that it went off very well, slept tight and when Mr. Chand got up in the morning, it was in the nick of the office going time. In the quickest few minutes, Mr. Chand readied himself and ran to the garage such that he could reach till the morning meeting, not being late. His eyes popped out seeing something most absurd to be precise...!! His car had been shifted diagonally across...if it was moved to the front, it would hit the garage post...if moved back, it would hit the bungalow wall...!! The car was trapped and its movements grounded...!! Feeling sweaty, Mr. Chand looked out for cars in the lane for a lift but alas, by then, everyone had already left for the office... Tensed up, he phoned the Boss, Field Superintendent... "Sir, Good Morning, I have landed up in a peculiar-most problem and walking to the office, will be few minutes late, excuse me please...!"

Boss: "OK, come fast...!!"

The meeting got over in its shortest set time and everyone moved out except Mr. Chand.

Boss asked what was his problem. He explained how his car had been moved to an awkward position by someone that it cannot be driven out from the garage...!!

Boss, with his momentary sharpness of thought, asked, "Did you invite everyone from your lane to your party last night...?"

Mr. Chand: Yes Sir, except for the two bachelors...!!

Boss: "OK, let me find out from admin a little more on it, you see me before you go for lunch break..."

Mr. Chand entered the Boss's Office near lunchtime.

Boss: "You go and meet the two bachelors now, promise them a bottle of whisky and some invitation later, they will fix the problem of your car...!!"

Taking a lift, Mr. Chand reached the bungalow shared by Bimal Hazarika and Rohiteswar Saikia, the two Machos from mighty Drilling Department..!!

Bimal Hazarika: "So you had a grand party, last night... we got the aroma and could hear the sounds of joys...!!"

Mr. Chand: "Arre Bimal, mere dost, Marriage Anniversary tha, isliye tum dono bachelors ko nahi invite kiya thaa... par main promise karta hoon, shaam ko ek bottle whisky bhejowa dunga...and we will have dinner together sometime later... Maaf karo yaar aur mera gaddi seedha kar do...!!"

Bimal Hazarika: "Whisky 750 ml ka hona hoga...!!"

Mr. Chand: Haan Jee, mere dost...!"

Both the machos, Bimal and Rohiteswar go to Mr. Chand's garage, lift the car by sheer muscle power and place it back in the right position for easy in and out movements...!!

Mr. Chand's eyes popped out further this time seeing the might of the two bachelors in action...!!

Such were the pranks, well-fought sports, fun and joys of True Friendship.

A band of Executives true to their profession, dedicated to the company with pure love was the essence that made Oil India Limited an Organization par Excellence...!!

(Jotted down the incident as I heard from my associates)

– *Ajit Mahanta*

Tribute by
Mr. Pradip Alley
Former OIL Indian
(Oil India Limited)

Bimal Kumar Hazarika: A Legend of
Drilling Industry of OIL (Oil India Limited)

His simplicity, devotion and work ethic were a great inspiration for many, including me. My first meeting with Bimal Hazarika was in an interview for drilling engineers with OIL.

I was a nervous youngster then. At first sight, Bimal Hazarika appeared to be an intimidating personality, but he could sense my nervousness and asked me to show my biceps in the interview. He made me comfortable and showed me his calm demeanor. After getting to know him better, it was obvious that he was a Man with a Golden Heart. His greatest quality was, he considered and loved everybody equally, without any difference. We all used to lovingly call him Bimal Dada (brother).

Bimal Dada was a distinguished leader in the field of Oil Drilling with many credits to his name.

He was a Born Driller. Back then, many notable performances of Drilling Operations in the Oil Industry were either credited to him or to his team.

His experience and knowledge in operations were commendable.

He was a visionary and his ability to understand and solve problematic situations was exceptional. I had the opportunity to work with him in such complicated operations.

I was amazed to realize his ability of perfect understanding and visualization of situations (especially 2-3 km depth), and solving the problems; particularly Oil Fishing Operations.

In mid-seventies, Bimal Dada married Arly Bou and lived as a "made for each other" lovely couple.

In my career, I was highly inspired by him and always looked up to him.

I am very proud to say that following his footsteps has led me to a successful Oil Fishing Career.

Lastly, I am grateful to Bimal Dada, as amidst many odds, he recommended my name for overseas Drilling Supervisor Training. That was the only overseas trip in my life.

Bimal Dada left for his heavenly abode many years ago, but he remains in my heart. I pray to God for his soul to Rest In Peace.

– Pradip Alley

THE UNIVERSE IS A STAGE, WE ALL ARE HERE TO PLAY DIFFERENT CHARACTERS. PLAY A ROLE IN YOUR LIFETIME WITH SUCH PASSION, THAT EVEN WHEN THE CURTAINS DROP, THE APPLAUSE DOESN'T STOP.

NOBODY AND NOTHING IS PERMANENT. MAKE A MARK WHILE ON YOUR EXISTENCE.

BE AN INSPIRATION FOR OTHERS TO FOLLOW.

THIS IS WHAT FATHER'S LIFE TAUGHT ME.

Chapter Eleven

Album

After his retirement in 1993 from Oil India Limited, he worked for North Eastern Drilling Pvt Ltd & Flotech Consultants as an Additional Director.

For an undoubted passion for his work, Father wanted to have his own Drilling Pvt Ltd, where he could still continue to live and keep exploring his love for Crude Oil Drilling. His own Company got registered in April 1997 but it never went to the floors as unfortunately, just a few months later, in September 1997, he was diagnosed with stage 4 cancer and he passed away in July 1998.

AN UNFULFILLED DREAM

"IF your actions inspire others to dream, learn more, do more, become more, you are a leader."

- John Quincy Adams

Binita Hazarika Dutta

**Explaining to his team at work in one1 of the well sites.
Approximate time: 1960s**

Approximate time of the picture: 80s beginning, probably at the Andamans

"Team Work is the ability to work together towards a common vision. The ability to direct individual accomplishments toward organizational objectives. It is a fuel that allows common people to attain uncommon results."

- Andrew Carnegie

Celebration on the occasion of winning in Deep Drilling 1988 Kud Location

"Excellence is never an accident. It is the result of high intention, sincere effort, intelligent direction, skillful execution & the vision to see the obstacles as opportunities."

- Aristotle

In England late 70 approx in England

Any Ritual Is An Opportunity For Transformation

Unity is strenghth..when there is team work& collaboration, wonderful things can be achieved.

Mattie Stepanek

No Info of the pic..either in Houstan Germany or England with his team.

The Success of Team Work

Coming together is a beginning

keeping together is progress

Working together is success

---Henry Ford--

The price of success is hard work, dedication to the job at hand, & determination that whether we win or loose, we have applied the best of ourselves to the task at hand

Vinci Lombardi

The End